# Balaam and the Talking Donkey

## Unusual Bible Stories

Written by Dr. Angel and Dan Mesman

Illustrated by Katie and Sunny Beebe

ISBN: 979-8-35094-227-9

# Preface: *Paw Paw and Me*

When I was a little girl, I enjoyed my grandfather's company. My husband and I wrote our first book: *Rudolph Remembers Stories of a Small Louisiana Town in the Early 1900s* to honor my Paw Paw Penton. In my case, I had caring parents, but I also had the pleasure of having a loving relationship with my grandfather. He was a storyteller with lots of patience for me and his other grandchildren!

The purpose of this book is for parents or grandparents to bond with their child or grandchild as they read the book to them. It's also an educational tool to teach your child a Biblical world view.

# Introduction

Paw Paw Rudolph enjoys sitting on his front porch with his granddaughter, Angel, who is seven years old. Sometimes, Paw Paw tells Angel stories of when he was a child growing up. He tells her how things were when he was younger. Other times, Paw Paw plays his banjo while singing Christian hymns such as "The Old Rugged Cross" or Hee Haw songs, and music such as "Shall We Gather at the River."

Angel's favorite times spent with her grandfather are when he reads her stories from the Bible. She climbs up on Paw Paw's lap as he holds the Bible and reads to her. This story is from the book, *Balaam and the Talking Donkey*.

[See more information in the back of the book.]

1

# Paw Paw and Angel on the Front Porch

Paw Paw and Angel are sitting on Paw Paw's front porch which is an Acadian style home. Acadian style homes were houses that were built to copy the houses of Acadians (French people from Nova Scotia) who settled in Louisiana in 1755. Paw Paw is seated on his rocking chair with his Bible in his hands. Angel is sitting on the steps of the porch, but comes to sit in her grandfather's lap.

Paw Paw: "Angel, what story from the Bible would you like me to read to you today?"

Angel: "Last Sunday, my children's church teacher told me there is a story in Numbers 22 about a talking animal. Could you read that story to me, Paw Paw?"

Paw Paw: Sure. Let me see. Numbers 22 is in the fourth book of the Old Testament in the Bible. Here it is!

# King Balak's Plans against God's People

The king of the Moabites, King Balak, heard that Moses and God's people, who were great in number, were coming to his country. King Balak was afraid because there were so many of them. Also, he heard about the many miracles that God performed to protect His people. God had parted the Red Sea so that they could cross and the army that was after them died in the sea when God's people were safely on the other side.

King Balak could see the fire that went before God's people at night to guide them and keep them warm in the chilly wilderness nights and the cloud that provided shade for them during the day from the scorching heat. One of his messengers had brought strange news of a Rock that followed God's people and two times water had flowed from the Rock!

King Balak sent a messenger to Balaam to pray for harm to come to God's people.

[See more information in the back of the book.]

# Balaam, God's Prophet Hears the Message

King Balak of the Moabites, enemy of God's people, sent messengers to tell Balaam, "Come at once. Curse this people for me, for they are too mighty for me. Perhaps I shall be able to defeat them and drive them out of the land, for I know that he whom you bless is blessed, and he whom you curse is cursed." The king told the men to promise Balaam that he would be paid for his services.

[See more information in the back of the book.]

# Balaam Prays to God for the First Time

When the men of Moab arrive at Balaam's home, Balaam asks them to stay the night while he talks to God and asks Him to curse His own people. Balaam's prayer to God: "Lord, King Balak has sent messengers to me. They say the people have come out of Egypt, and they cover the face of the earth. Come now, curse them for me; perhaps I will be able to overpower them and drive them out."

God answers Balaam, "You shall not go with them; you shall not curse the people, for they are blessed!!"

The next morning, Balaam told King Balak's men, "Go back to your land, for the LORD has refused to give me permission to go with you." So they went back home and told King Balak what Balaam said.

# God Speaks to Us

Angel: "Paw Paw, can we talk to God just like Balaam talked to God? "

Paw Paw: "Yes, that is what prayer is. In prayer, we can praise God for who He is, thank Him for all the ways He has blessed us, and ask Him for guidance and protection. He usually answers our prayer by putting peaceful thoughts in our head and heart, giving us dreams and songs, or as we read our Bible and listen to sermons, He encourages us so that we know that He is speaking to us through the pastor's words or Bible verses."

"God always answers prayer. Sometimes, the answer is "Yes". Other times the answer is "No". Also, the answer can be "Wait". God loves us and wants us to stay close to Him every day. Let's read more of the story."

# King Balak Tries Again

King Balak refused to quit! He sent lots of honorable men to Balaam the second time to change his mind. They told Balaam, "Thus says Balak: 'Please let nothing keep you from coming to me; for I will certainly honor you greatly, and I will do whatever you say to me. Therefore, please come, curse this people for me'".

Balaam replied, "Though Balak were to give me a house full of silver and gold, I would not go beyond the word of the LORD, my God, to do less or more. Stay the night and I will talk to God."

God told Balaam, "If the men come to call you, rise and go with them; but only say what I tell you to say". The next morning, Balaam saddled his donkey and went with King Balak's men.

# Does God Change His Mind?

Angel: "Paw Paw, why did God say the first time not to go, then the second time He said, 'Go?' Does God change His mind?"

Paw Paw: "Angel, sometimes God does change His mind. In the story of the angels who come to destroy the cities of Sodom and Gomorrah, Abraham prayed that God would spare the city if there were 50 righteous (good) people living in the city. He continued asking God to spare the city until God agreed not to destroy the city if there were 10 righteous people living in the city."

In the story of Balaam, God was testing Balaam's heart. God always loves us and He wants us to love Him back. Let's continue the story.

[See more information in the back of the book.]

# *Balaam's Donkey Sees An Angel*

Then God's anger was aroused because Balaam went, and the Angel of the LORD took His stand in the way as an adversary against Balaam. The donkey Balaam was riding saw the Angel of the LORD standing in the way with His sword drawn in His hand, so the donkey turned aside out of the way and went into the field. So Balaam struck the donkey with his staff to turn her back onto the road.

[See more information in the back of the book.]

# Why Did Only the Donkey See the Angel?

Angel: "Paw Paw, don't you find this story unusual! The donkey saw the angel but Balaam didn't."

Paw Paw: "Yes, Angel, Balaam was so set on doing what the king asked rather than what God had told him that he did not see an angel. Some people are more interested in money, than being faithful to God. Balaam was going against God's will."

# *Balaam's Donkey Sees the Angel Again*

Then the Angel of the LORD stood in a narrow path between the vineyards with a wall on this side and a wall on that side. When the donkey saw the Angel of the LORD, she pushed herself against the wall and crushed Balaam's foot against the wall; so Balaam struck the donkey again.

# A Girl Donkey

Angel: "Paw Paw, I feel sad for the donkey. She was saving herself and Balaam from harm, but Balaam kept hitting her. The donkey was a girl. Let's give her a name."

Paw Paw: "Ok. I remember when you rode a pony at a birthday party. The owners had a farm. On the farm they also had a donkey named Deborah. She was named after the Bible story in Judges 4. Let's call the donkey in this story Deborah, since she doesn't have a name."

[See more information in the back of the book.]

# Deborah, the Donkey Talks

Then the Angel of the LORD went further and stood in a narrow place where there was no way to turn either to the right hand or to the left. When Deborah, the donkey, saw the Angel of the LORD, she lay down under Balaam; so Balaam's anger was aroused, and he struck the donkey with his staff.

Then the LORD opened the mouth of Deborah, the donkey, and she said to Balaam, "What have I done to you, that you have struck me these three times?"

Balaam said to the donkey, "Because you have hurt me. I wish there were a sword in my hand, for now I would kill you!"

Deborah, the donkey, said to Balaam, "Am I not your donkey on which you have ridden all your life? Have I ever done this to you before? Balaam said, "No!"

26

# *Balaam Sees the Angel of the LORD*

Then Balaam's eyes were opened, and he saw the Angel of the LORD standing in the way with His drawn sword in His hand, and Balaam bowed his head and fell flat on his face.

[See more information in the back of the book.]

# Angel of the LORD is Jesus

Angel: "Paw Paw, why would Balaam bow down to an angel?"

Paw Paw: "Well, the Bible describes Jesus as the Angel of the LORD, so Balaam was bowing down to worship Jesus! One day when we get to heaven, the angels and believers—that's us along with many other Christians—will be praising and worshipping God, the Father, the Son, and the Holy Spirit!"

[See more information in the back of the book.]

# Jesus Speaks to Balaam

The Angel of the LORD (Jesus) said, "Why have you struck your donkey those three times? I have come to block your way, because you are not listening to Me."

Jesus continues, "The donkey saw Me and turned away from Me these three times. If she had not turned away from Me, surely I would also have killed you by now, and let her live."

Balaam said to Jesus, "I have sinned, for I did not know You stood in the road to block me. I'll go home if you want me to."

Jesus told Balaam, "Go with the men, but only say what I tell you to say."

So Balaam went with King Balak's men.

# God Loves Everyone

Angel: "Paw Paw, I just love Jesus! He could have killed Balaam but he didn't. Jesus loved Balaam, huh, Paw Paw?"

Paw Paw: "Yes, Angel, John 3:16 says that He loves everyone and wants them to go to heaven with Him.

Angel: "Please read the verse to me?"

Paw Paw: "For God so loved the world, that He gave His only begotten Son and whosoever believes in Him shall not perish but have everlasting life."

Angel: "My children's church teacher says that we can say a prayer of salvation."

Paw Paw: "Yes, Angel, If people say this prayer and mean it, then they will be saved."

Prayer:

*Dear Jesus, thank You for dying on the Cross for me. Forgive me of my sins. Be the Lord over my life. Help me to live in a way that honors You. Amen.*

# Balaam Sacrifices on the High Mountain

When King Balak heard that Balaam was coming, he met Balaam at the city of Moab. He brought Balaam to the high mountain so they could observe the multitude of God's people below.

Balaam said to King Balak, "Have your servants build seven altars for me, and prepare for me here seven bulls and seven rams. A sacrifice was made on all the altars.

# Jesus, the Lamb of God

Angel: "Paw Paw, why did people in the Old Testament kill animals as worship to God?"

Paw Paw: "Well, Jesus is called the Lamb of God. He died for our sins on the Cross. When the people sacrificed the animals on the altar, they did knowing that one day their Savior would remove their sins and they would one day be with Jesus in heaven.

Angel: "Please, read more, Paw Paw!"

# Balaam Blesses God's People

Balaam prayed to God. God told Balaam to say, "How shall I curse whom God has not cursed?"

King Balak said to Balaam, "What have you done? I told you to curse God's people and you have blessed them, greatly!"

Balaam replied, "I speak what God tells me." King Balak asked Balaam to go to another place where he could see some of God's people from afar and try again to pray to bring them harm.

# Two More Times

Two more times seven altars were built and animals were sacrificed on the altars. Balaam met with God. God told Balaam to say, "God is not a man, so He does not lie. Has He ever spoken, and failed to act? Has He ever promised, and not carried it through? Listen, I have received a command to bless; God has blessed, and I cannot reverse it."

King Balak was angry but Balaam spoke only the words the Lord gave him to speak.

# Moral of the Story

Angel: "So Paw Paw, was Balaam a good man?"

Paw Paw: "Even though in the end Balaam seemed obedient, his whole purpose in going with King Balak was to make himself rich rather than honor Jesus and what Jesus had told him."

Angel: "Paw Paw, I love when you read to me stories from the Bible."

Paw Paw: "I'm so glad that you want to learn about the Bible. Every Christian should read their Bible daily because it helps them make good choices in life!"

— THE END —

# Endnotes

This information refers to the **introduction page one**:

Hee Haw music was similar to country gospel music with banjos, guitars, tamborines, and harmonicas used for instruments and usually a quartet of singers harmonizing. The Wikipedia definition of four part harmony of the gospel quartet (similar to Hee Haw music) is tenor, or the highest part; lead, which usually takes the melody; baritone, which blends the sounds and adds richness; and the bass, or the lowest part.

This information refers to **page five**: King Balak's Plans Against God's People

Who was Balaam? **Numbers 22:5** says that Balaam was the son of Beor at Pethor, which is near the River Euphrates in the land of the sons of his people, Amau. Balaam was a non-Israelite prophet or seer.

This information refers to **page seven:** Balaam God's Prophet Hears the Message

What is a curse? According to the dictionary, a curse is a prayer or invocation (calling upon God) for harm or injury to come upon someone; in this case, God's people.

This information refers to **page fifteen**: Does God Change His Mind?

The definition of a righteous person is one who lives according to God's commands and divine laws. A person who lives free from guilt or sin is a righteous person.

This information refers to **page seventeen**: Balaam's Donkey Sees An Angel

The Angel of the Lord was Jesus. The description in **Numbers 22:23** says, "the donkey saw the Angel of the LORD standing in the way with His drawn sword in His hand."

How do we know this? Because people do not bow down and worship angels. *Later on page 13, Balaam bows down to the Angel of the Lord.*

This information refers to **page twenty-three**: A Girl Donkey

Reference to Deborah in **Judges 4**.

Deborah was a prophetess who judged the people of Israel in Old Testament times when God's people had disobeyed Him. Because they disobeyed God, He had allowed the Canaanites to invade their land. King Hazor of the Canaanites had a mighty army that oppressed God's people. Deborah told Barak that God had told her if he and his men fought against the Canaanites, then Barak and God's people would win. Barak said that he would not go to fight unless Deborah went also. Deborah went. God brought a mighty victory for God's people.

How do we know that the donkey was a girl?

**Numbers 22:25** says, "And when the donkey saw the Angel of the LORD, **she** pushed **herself** against the wall and crushed Balaam's foot against the wall; so he struck **her** again."

This information refers to **page twenty-seven**: Balaam Sees the Angel of the LORD

Why were people told by God not to bow down to men or angels?

In the Old Testament, God gave His people rules or commands to help guide them in making good life decisions. In **Exodus 23:24** (God was instructed His people not to worship the gods of other lands.)"You shall not bow down to their gods." Also, in the ten commandments, **Exodus 20:3** God says, "You shall have no other gods before Me."

This information refers to **page twenty-nine**: Angel of the LORD is Jesus

When did Jesus appear as an Angel of the Lord in the Bible?

Jesus appears in the Old Testament as an Angel of God. Here are four stories in the Bible where Jesus gives instructions to His people:

- In Genesis 18: 1 & 2 Abraham was visited by the Lord Jesus before the angels visited Sodom and Gomorrah.
- In Genesis 32 Jacob is desperately holding onto Jesus for a blessing.
- In Judges 6 the Lord gives Gideon a plan to defeat the Midianites..
- In Judges 13 Manoah and his wife were visited by the Angel of the Lord.